1·8

WEEKLY WR READER®
EARLY LEARNING LIBRARY

Things with Wings

THE LIFE CYCLE OF A
FLAMINGO

by JoAnn Early Macken

Reading consultant: Susan Nations, M.Ed.,
author/literacy coach/consultant in literacy development

Please visit our web site at: www.earlyliteracy.cc
For a free color catalog describing Weekly Reader® Early Learning Library's
list of high-quality books, call 1-877-445-5824 (USA) or 1-800-387-3178 (Canada).
Weekly Reader® Early Learning Library's fax: (414) 336-0164.

Library of Congress Cataloging-in-Publication Data

Macken, JoAnn Early, 1953-
    The life cycle of a flamingo / by JoAnn Early Macken.
       p. cm. — (Things with wings)
    Includes index.
    ISBN 0-8368-6382-8 (lib. bdg.)
    ISBN 0-8368-6389-5 (softcover)
    1. Flamingos—Life cycles—Juvenile literature. I. Title.
QL696.C56M23 2006
598.3'5—dc22   2005026542

This edition first published in 2006 by
Weekly Reader® Early Learning Library
A Member of the WRC Media Family of Companies
330 West Olive Street, Suite 100
Milwaukee, WI 53212 USA

Copyright © 2006 by Weekly Reader® Early Learning Library

Managing editor: Dorothy L. Gibbs
Art direction: Tammy West
Photo research: Diane Laska-Swanke

Photo credits: Cover, p. 11 © Tom and Pat Leeson; pp. 5, 9, 21 © Solvin Zankl/naturepl.com;
p. 7 © Doug Allan/naturepl.com; p. 13 © Dave Watts/naturepl.com; p. 15 © Peter Blackwell/
naturepl.com; p. 17 © Paul Hobson/naturepl.com; p. 19 © Anup Shah/naturepl.com

Printed in the United States of America

1 2 3 4 5 6 7 8 9 10 09 08 07 06

Note to Educators and Parents

Reading is such an exciting adventure for young children! They are beginning to integrate their oral language skills with written language. To encourage children along the path to early literacy, books must be colorful, engaging, and interesting; they should invite the young reader to explore both the print and the pictures.

Things with Wings is a new series designed to help children read about fascinating animals, all of which have wings. In each book, young readers will learn about the life cycle of the featured animal, as well as other interesting facts.

Each book is specially designed to support the young reader in the reading process. The familiar topics are appealing to young children and invite them to read — and re-read — again and again. The full-color photographs and enhanced text further support the student during the reading process.

In addition to serving as wonderful picture books in schools, libraries, homes, and other places where children learn to love reading, these books are specifically intended to be read within an instructional guided reading group. This small group setting allows beginning readers to work with a fluent adult model as they make meaning from the text. After children develop fluency with the text and content, the book can be read independently. Children and adults alike will find these books supportive, engaging, and fun!

— Susan Nations, M.Ed., author, literacy coach, and consultant in literacy development

A baby flamingo, or **chick**, hatches from an egg. Its soft feathers are gray. Its neck and legs are long.

Flamingo chicks know their parents by their voices. Flamingos honk like geese.

A flamingo parent feeds its chicks until the chicks can find their own food. In about one week, a chick leaves the nest for the first time. After about three months, the chick can fly.

nest

9

A flamingo's beak curves down. Flamingos eat with their heads upside down in the water. They trap tiny plants and animals in their beaks.

11

All flamingos are pink. Some are light, and some are dark. The pink color comes from their food. Their wings and beaks are partly black.

beak

wing

13

Flamingos live in warm places.
Most live near salty lakes. They
use their webbed feet to swim.
They may dive to find food.

Flamingos can sleep standing up. They often stand on one leg. A flamingo may also tuck its head under one wing.

Flamingos form large groups called **flocks**. All the birds in a flock stay close to each other. They build their nests close to each other, too.

Flamingos make nests out of mud. Most of the time, each nest holds only one egg. Each pair of birds raises one chick. A flamingo can live for forty years.

egg

21

The Life Cycle of a Flamingo

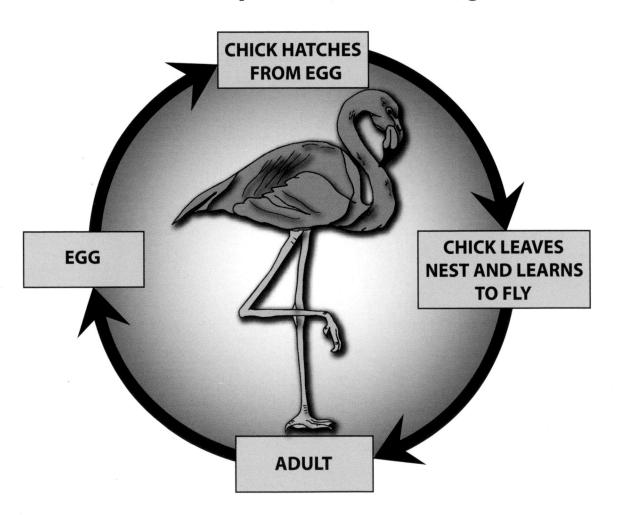

Glossary

chick — a baby bird

flocks — large groups of birds

hatches — breaks out of an egg

webbed — having toes that are joined together by skin

Index

About the Author

JoAnn Early Macken is the author of two rhyming picture books, *Sing-Along Song* and *Cats on Judy*, and more than eighty nonfiction books for children. Her poems have appeared in several children's magazines. A graduate of the M.F.A. in Writing for Children and Young Adults Program at Vermont College, she lives in Wisconsin with her husband and their two sons.